HARBI GANI

(How are you?)

MAMA, BABA AND MPENDWA

(Loved one!)

Our Love for Mommy was created to show Black mothers appreciation for all they do for their children and families. We want Black mothers of all kinds—single, married, adoptive or cultural—to know we truly appreciate you! You are the reason our children and families stay intact!

This book was also created because we believe Black fathers play a major role in teaching our sons how to show love and appreciation to Black women in general and Black mothers specifically. Our sons need to see regular, open displays of Black fathers honoring, respecting, and showing love to Black mothers and Black women. They also need to hear Black fathers tell their wives and partners they love them regularly. In co-parenting situations, our sons need to be a part of and see their fathers having amicable relationships with their mothers, centered on respecting, valuing, and appreciating her.

Black fathers also play a major role in teaching our children how to share family and household responsibilities with their mothers or significant other. Our sons need to work with their fathers to learn to cook, clean, take care of their siblings, pay bills, and take care of other responsibilities in the home. They need to see their fathers working and coordinating those responsibilities with their mother or significant other. **Our Love for Mommy** shares the things a Black father and son love about the Black woman in their life.

WE HOPE YOU ENJOY THE STORY!

One morning, Daddy and Sekou dropped Mommy off at the United States of Africa Airport for a flight to North Carolina. When they arrived, Daddy got out of the car and removed Mommy's suitcase from the trunk. Mommy grabbed her purse and got out of the car.

UNITED STATES

Mommy opened the car door and reached inside to give Sekou a big hug and kiss. "Love you!" she said with a big smile. Then, she turned to Daddy and gave him a hug and a kiss, too.

"I love you," Daddy said.

"I love you, too!" Mommy said.

Mommy grabbed her suitcase from Daddy and waved goodbye to her family. "Bye, Mommy, I love you!" Sekou blurted out as Mommy walked away.

Mommy turned around and waved goodbye. "I love you, too, Sekou. See you when I get back!"

Daddy and Sekou got back in the car and started driving home.

"I'm going to miss, Mommy," Sekou said sadly.

"I am going to miss Mommy, too! But do not worry, she will be back soon," Daddy reassured Sekou.

BLACK STAR LINE
TRUCKING COMPANY
TAKING CHARGE OF OUR ECONOMIC FREEDO

Daddy and Sekou drove in silence for a few minutes. Then, seemingly out of no-where, Sekou asked, "Why do you love Mommy?"

Daddy looked at Sekou in the rearview mirror. "That is a good question, Sekou. My love for your mother developed many years ago when we were dating, before you were even born."

"Really, Daddy?" replied Sekou as he tried to imagine Mommy and Daddy dating before he was born.

Daddy explained further. "Your mother is a good woman with a loving heart and outgoing personality. She has a way of getting people to love her by simply being herself—a quality that I really love!"

"All of my brothers and sisters at school really like Mommy, too. They think she is nice. They like her lappas and they enjoy her cooking," said Sekou.

Daddy and Sekou arrived home safely. Daddy helped Sekou out of his car seat and they walked into the house.

Daddy hung his keys on the rack near the door.
They continued to discuss all the reasons why
Daddy loved Mommy.

"Your mother has always supported me in everything I do. She supported me when I was working to further my education. I know she loves me and wants the best for me. She makes me a better man, husband, and father," said Daddy.

Sekou replied, "I know Mommy loves me and wants the best for me, too! How did Mommy make you a better man, husband, and father?"

"Your mother is a really smart woman who makes me think more and offers ideas I never thought about. She gave me ideas about how to better manage my time to do more for Black boys in our community. I feel like those ideas have made me a better man," replied Daddy.

Manhood Development Program

Preparing African boys to be African men

Institution Building

African manhood

Sovereignty

Nation Building

Weekly

Liberation

Babas facilitating manhood sessions

Sekou chimed in. "Mommy is really smart. She helps me with my family work and always teaches me new things! She taught me how to read, write and count. How did Mommy help you become a better husband?"

"Well, she taught me that marriage is about give and take, and one person can't always be the one giving. Most Black women tend to be givers and they are willing to do anything for the people they love. Your mother taught me that we both must be willing to give to make our marriage and family work. That has made me more open-minded, patient and understanding," explained Daddy.

"Daddy, I didn't think about it like that. I will remember not to take Mommy's love and all she does for me for granted. I have to be willing to give and do for her, too!" said Sekou.

"Yes, you're right, Sekou." Daddy said.

Daddy walked into the kitchen to make breakfast. They continued their conversation at the table. "I still want to know how Mommy made you a better father," Sekou said.

"Your mother made me a better man, husband, and father when we conceived you," Daddy said. "Having a son is a blessing and comes with a lot of responsibility. Mothers and fathers must make sure their sons are raised to be good men, husbands, and fathers in the future," explained Daddy.

"Mommy made sure her body was taken care of for me to have a healthy birth. I am thankful to mommy for going through all the changes with her body to make sure I was born healthy. I am also thankful that she breastfed me," said Sekou.

"Your mother has also helped me to be more conscious and reflective of the things I say and do around you. I want to set a good example for you. Your mother keeps me grounded and focused on being a good father to you and a good husband to her," explained Daddy as they finished their breakfast.

"Daddy, mommy is a really special lady," said Sekou.

"Yes, she is, Sekou. She is a very special lady. That is why I love her," said Daddy.

"I love Mommy, too, Daddy," said Sekou.

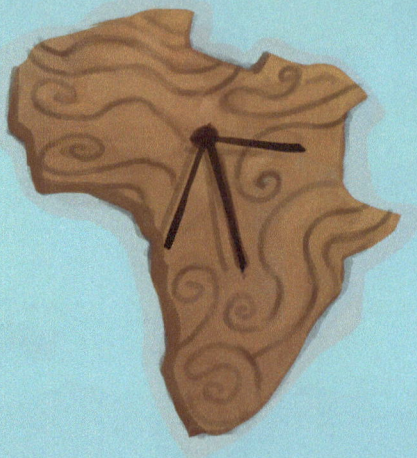

Daddy and Sekou headed into the family room to play Black History Bingo. As Daddy called out the names of Black history figures, they each placed chips on their boards when they had a match.

After a few minutes of playing the game, Sekou called out, "Black History Bingo" to signal that he had filled one row on his board with chips. Daddy checked Sekou's board to make sure he'd done it correctly. He confirmed that Sekou won the game.

"Good job!" Daddy said. "Now let's clean up the game so we can read a story." Sekou loved reading stories with Daddy.

A few hours later, Daddy's cell phone rang. It was Mommy calling to say she had arrived safely.

MAMA

Sekou was glad Mommy called. "Can I talk to her?" he asked excitedly. Daddy smiled and handed Sekou the phone.

BINGO

FREEDOM
AFRICA
FREEDOM
KINGS
AFRICA
AFRICA
RIGHTS
JAZZ
EQUALITY
JAZZ
AFRICA
JAZZ

BLACK HISTORY BINGO

Sekou grabbed the phone from Daddy and with a big smile on his face, he said, "I love and appreciate you, Mommy!"

Mommy was not expecting to hear that from Sekou. His words warmed her heart and made her smile. "Thank you, Sekou," she said. "What made you say that?"

Sekou said, "Daddy and I were talking about our love for you and the need for us to share our feelings with you."

"That's nice of you and Daddy to talk about your love for me," she said.

"I appreciate you sharing your conversation and feelings with me. You made my day, Sekou. Alright, I got to go. I will call you and Daddy later. Bye, Sekou."

Zora Neale Hurston

Akwaaba

Our Love for Mommy

Our love for mommy

...is real

...it comes with no strings attached

Mommy is the

greatest creation the Creator

ever made - A true reflection of Divinity

Mommy is a creator and

nurturer of precious valuable

Black life

Mommy is a selfless giver

to her children, helpmate, family,

race, and community to build a

Black nation

Mommy is an intelligent, hardworking,

and humble Black woman who does

not need or desire recognition

for the seeds she sows

Mommy is a natural

teacher and cultivator of

knowledge

Our Love for Mommy

...extends beyond words

and deeds and runs

deep in our soul

Baba Sekou Afrika   Sekou Afrika

CULTURALLY UPLIFTING FAMILY WORK!

BLACK FAMILIES should engage regularly in culturally uplifting learning activities that strengthen and help our families learn and experience new things together. We humbly present the culturally uplifting learning activities and experiences for you to engage in by yourself, with your children, cultural children, and members of your family:

1. Self-Assessment: From childhood to adulthood, reflect on your relationship with your mother, grandmothers, aunts, cousins, and women in your family. Think about the ways you show love to Black women in your life. Do your ways of showing love represent how you want the important women in your life to experience your love? Do you show your love explicitly (clear and obvious) or implicitly (not stated)? How do the women in your life know you love them? After reflecting on how you show your love, make sure you show the important women in your life love in a way that lets them know you love them.

2. Tell your mother, grandmothers, aunts, and important women in your life that you love them every time you see them and encourage your son to do the same.

3. Read your son poems and/or books daily that positively depicts Black women, families, and children and discuss it with him.

4. Create father-and-son dates with mommy, where you bring her flowers and take her out to places she likes.

5. Buy father-and-son gifts for mommy on her birthday.

6. Teach your son about strong Black women in your family and in our culture in Africa, the Americas, Caribbean and Diaspora.

7. Post artwork of strong Black women around your house.

ABOUT THE AUTHORS

Family Afrika is a Black family that lives in Baltimore, Maryland. They believe in the importance of Black families and children connecting, honoring and respecting our cultural heritage and traditions in Africa, America, the Caribbean, and the Diaspora. As a family, we work hard to learn about our cultural heritage and traditions. We practice the Nguzo Saba (The 7 Principles of Blackness) in our everyday lives and give back to our community.

The stories presented in our books are fictionalized accounts based on real events in our family and our journey to live a life that connects, honors, and respects our cultural heritage and traditions. Reading should be a regular occurrence in Black families, and it is important for Black children to see images that look like them in the books they read.

Becoming parents and watching our son, Sekou, grow up inspired these books and the stories in them. Sekou is a co-author because he has contributed greatly to the books. Mama and Baba use his name as co-authors of the books to honor his contributions. We use Afrika as our last name to represent our quest to positively uplift our cultural heritage and traditions originating in Africa. Sekou inspired us to live a life that more closely reflects our beliefs and political ideology. We strongly believe we have to create Black institutions to positively uplift Black families and children, and connect them to their cultural heritage and traditions.

BABA SEKOU AFRIKA, ED.D. (also known as Julius Davis) is an associate professor of mathematics education at Bowie State University. His scholarship and advocacy focuses on the intellectual and social development of Black boys and young men. He has studied and traveled to Malawi, Tanzania, and Ethiopia on the continent of Africa to learn more about our cultural heritage and traditions.

MAMA SEKOU AFRIKA (also known as Yolanda Davis) is a clinical research professional who has studied and traveled to Senegal on the continent of Africa and the Caribbean Islands to learn more about our cultural heritage and traditions.

SEKOU AFRIKA (also known as Sekou Davis) is a student at Ujamaa Shule, the oldest independent Afrikan School in the United States. He plays the Afrikan drums with his brothers and sisters at Ujamaa. To start his formal school-based academic and social development, Sekou attended Watoto Development Center in Baltimore, MD, an Afrikan-centered institution.

Asante Sana (Thank you very much) for practicing **Ujamaa** (cooperative economics) by purchasing this book and supporting our Black-owned family business.

A portion of the proceeds from this book will be used to support and sponsor efforts to culturally uplift Black children and families.

Your Support is Greatly Appreciated!

Baba Sekou Afrika, Mama Sekou Afrika, Sekou Afrika

KUJICHAGULIA PRESS

We define, speak and create for ourselves to celebrate our African and African American cultural heritage and uplift our people using our Kuumba (creativity).

Title: Our Love For Mommy
Written by: Baba Sekou Afrika, Mama Sekou Afrika, and Sekou Afrika
Edited By: Nadirah Angail

Summary: Our Love for Mommy was created to show Black mothers appreciation for all they do for their children and families.

ISBN: 978-0-9964595-8-7

For more information or to book an event, contact Baba/Mama Sekou at books@kujichaguliapress.com.

Kujichagulia Press
P.O. Box 31766
Baltimore, MD 21207
www.kujichaguliapress.com

KujichaguliaPress   KujichaguliaPress   @Kujichaguliaprs

#OurLoveForMommy
#ILoveMommy
#MommyLovesYou
#ILoveYou

www.ingramcontent.com/pod-product-compliance
Lightning Source LLC
Chambersburg PA
CBHW041556040426

42447CB00002B/184